A 30-DAY DEVOTIONAL

C H O S E N

WHAT WOULD HAPPEN IF YOU REMINDED YOURSELF
OF THE GOSPEL EVERY DAY?

RYAN SKOOG AND MATT BROWN

OUTREΛCH®

Chosen

© 2018 by Outreach, Inc.

Published by Outreach, Inc., Colorado Springs, CO 80919
www.Outreach.com

Unless otherwise noted, Scripture quotations in this publication are taken from THE HOLY BIBLE, NEW INTERNATIONAL VERSION®, NIV® Copyright © 1973, 1978, 1984, 2011 by Biblica, Inc.® Used by permission. All rights reserved worldwide. Also used is the ESV® Bible (The Holy Bible, English Standard Version®). ESV® Text Edition: 2016. Copyright © 2001 by Crossway, a publishing ministry of Good News Publishers. The ESV® text has been reproduced in cooperation with and by permission of Good News Publishers. Unauthorized reproduction of this publication is prohibited. All rights reserved; the NEW AMERICAN STANDARD BIBLE® (NASB), Copyright © 1960, 1962,1963,1968,1971,1972,1973,1975,1977,1995 by The Lockman Foundation. Used by permission; the Holy Bible, New Living Translation (NLT), copyright © 1996, 2004, 2007, 2013, 2015 by Tyndale House Foundation. Used by permission of Tyndale House Publishers, Inc., Carol Stream, Illinois 60188. All rights reserved; and the King James Version (KJV).

ISBN: 9781635107265
Cover Design by Tim Downs
Interior Design by Alexia Garaventa
Written by Matt Brown and Ryan Skoog
Program Manager: Erica Chumbley

Printed in the United States of America

To our parents —
Tim and Melody,
Mark and Tami
— who intentionally shared the Gospel with us at a
young age and continue to practice resurrection in
their daily lives.

And to our children —
Caden and Jordan,
Colin and Sydney
— may you know the supreme joy in life that comes
from knowing the Lord and preaching the Gospel
to your own heart every day.

CONTENTS

ENDORSEMENTS

"Matt and Ryan shed light on a life-changing question: how might our lives be different if we took time every day to intentionally focus our hearts and minds on the Gospel? Through rich story-telling they invite pastors, ministry leaders, and all Christ-followers to awaken to the power of the Gospel, reminding them that the Gospel transforms our lives every day. This is a book you will not only read for yourself, but share with many others as a gift of encouragement on their journey with Jesus."

—Jason Daye, Host of the ChurchLeaders podcast, Director of ministry partnerships at Outreach

"One of the greatest promises in the Bible is knowing that we are chosen by God. That the Creator of the universe chooses us! You and me. What does that fully mean? This book is for you. Matt Brown and Ryan Skoog explain the Gospel and what it simply yet fully means to be chosen by God."

—Adam Weber, Pastor & Author of *Talking With God*

"The most transformative message to reach our lives is the Gospel! I've personally experienced how easy it is to lose sight of the power and impact of this message, which is why this book is essential! The authors live the gospel and you can feel that on every page and in every story! Great for anyone just starting their walk with Jesus, new members, a series with your groups, or anyone wanting to stir up their spiritual passion again!"

—Samuel Deuth, speaker, author of *Following Jesus*

"Maybe we, as Jesus' followers, would get more excited about sharing his Gospel with others if we grasped it better ourselves. This delightful new devotional recounts story after powerful story to remind us of just how *GREAT* the Good News really is—for ourselves, and for everyone we know."

—Mark Mittelberg, primary author of the bestselling *Becoming a Contagious Christian* training course, and coauthor of *Making Your Case for Christ* (with Lee Strobel)

INTRODUCTION

What would happen if you woke up and reminded yourself of the Gospel every day?

If you are like me, you are tempted to take the Gospel for granted and stop rehearsing it because it's become so familiar. We store it in our story somewhere in the past and subconsciously try to move on from it. But we need to hear the Gospel every bit as much today as we did the day we heard it for the first time.

If we remind ourselves of the Gospel each morning, we will wake up and live in grateful joy that the toughest battle we are going to face today has already been won.

How different would your life be if you preached the Gospel to your own heart more regularly? Speaker and author Paul Tripp said, "Preach the gospel to yourself. No one is more influential in your life than you are. Because no one talks to you more than you do."

We wrote this book to help you influence yourself better—to talk to yourself more about Jesus.

BEST MORNING EVER

I believe the best way to change your life is simply to change your normal day. This is how reminding my soul of the Gospel every morning has changed my life:

- When I remember how God has included me in His family, I don't look for acceptance in everyone I meet throughout the day.

- When I remind myself of how passionately God loves me, I don't look for love from social-media "likes" or compliments throughout the day.

- When I realize I am blessed for all eternity, I don't seek happiness in other things or people.

- When I remind myself that I have been chosen by God, I don't go through the day looking for people's approval.

- When I remind my soul I have already won the most important victory ever, I don't base my self-worth on accomplishing every goal, impressing every person, or winning every argument.

- When I realize that God has given me His complete attention because of Christ, I don't go around seeking people's attention.

- When I realize the price Jesus paid to set me free, I don't have to find my worth in things and titles. I don't have to find people to invite me into their circle; I've already been invited by God into His elect circle.

The result is joy. I walk through much more of my day in a state of grateful obedience—grateful for what Christ has done and wanting to obediently serve Him throughout the day.

This book will help you each morning to walk through these different gifts of the Gospel that can completely change the outlook of your day. And if you change your day, it can change your entire life.

THE BOOK BEHIND THIS BOOK

The Bible has much to say about the Gospel. If you want to learn to preach the Gospel to yourself, you have to let God's Word preach the Gospel to you. The Gospel is the story of Jesus Christ, who came to earth, lived a sinless life, gave His life on a brutal cross as a ransom for our sins, and rose from the dead three days later. He now sits at the right hand of the Father as the Name Above All Names. All of Scripture points to this Christ and this good news.

As different as we all are, we all need the same grace—the same Savior. We all deserve shame, wrath, and hell, but Jesus offers us grace, hope, and heaven. The Gospel beckons us to confess our sin and our need for Christ, and to believe in and receive what He did on the cross for us. When we do this, we become a child of God with countless spiritual benefits—benefits freely given by the grace and mercy of our Father.

And we will always need the Gospel. We do not get saved by the Gospel and then move on to discipleship, attempting to live our Christian lives out of our own power. The entirety of our Christian life is built on the Gospel. The Gospel not only saves us, it also sustains us throughout our lives. The Gospel fuels and motivates us to serve and obey God every step of the way. We will never be perfect, and so we will always rely on what Christ has done for us—which means we will always need to be reminded of what He has done for us.

Too many Christians are famished for the Gospel. Too many of us are living our lives without grasping the giant potential and overwhelming wonder of everything God does for us in the Gospel. Losing sight of the Gospel negatively affects our faith in countless ways. We need to preach and preach and preach the Gospel to our hearts—the Gospel we find in the Bible.

YOU NEVER OUTGROW THE GOSPEL

You probably haven't experienced all the benefits or "aspects" of the Gospel yet. There are dozens of ways the Gospel positively impacts and shapes our everyday lives. We all need regular reminders of these aspects and need God's power to grasp them more. If we don't understand the benefits, they can't change our lives or grow our faith.

The Gospel dramatically affects our daily lives. The Gospel is not some pie-in-the-sky theory; it's down-to-earth truth about Jesus that affects our real lives on a daily basis and influences us in profound ways. The Gospel has the power to change everything in our daily lives if we let it—our attitudes, our motivations, our desires, our goals, our actions, our interactions with others. This starts with preaching the Gospel to our own hearts—coming to understand it better, being reminded of it regularly, and letting it fill our hearts with wonder.

None of us has looked deeply enough. It's not that we have heard the Gospel too much; we haven't *really* heard it enough yet! Like many facets to a beautiful diamond, the Gospel has an infinite beauty that can never be exhausted. The more we look into the Gospel, the stronger and more satisfied we will be in our faith.

My grandfather-in-law was a pastor for fifty years, and he had the habit of reading the whole Bible every year. He would often say, "That verse was never in there before!" When we stay in God's Word, He will open up our hearts to different truths at different times, even while we read the same pages over and over. This Book meets us right where we are and speaks to us in just the way we need right now. As Charles Spurgeon, one of the most highly influential preachers of his time, said, "Nobody ever outgrows Scripture; the book widens and deepens with our years." It is the same with the Gospel story Scripture is telling—nobody ever outgrows the Gospel.

THE STORY BEHIND THIS BOOK

I met Ryan Skoog years ago when I was a student at summer camp. He was traveling in a band and also happened to be a counselor that week for me and a group of friends. I still remember the stories he shared each night about the Gospel transforming lives. Those stories were pivotal in my faith. They painted pictures in my imagination of just how powerful the Gospel really is.

Ryan and I have stayed in touch over the years and have enjoyed a friendship. About a year ago, Ryan approached me with the idea for this book, wanting to help Christians preach the Gospel to their hearts each day. This simple idea—rehearsing and meditating on the benefits of the Gospel—has changed our lives in profound ways. Our hope is that as you read, we can be camp counselors for you, sitting together around a campfire, inspiring you with real-life stories of how we've seen God working in people's lives through this incredible Gospel. We want you to see how regularly reminding your own heart of the Gospel can transform your walk with God.

We have written this book in a thirty-day format, with thirty benefits of the Gospel to preach to your own heart, all drawn from the Bible. But we also tell a lot of personal stories that illustrate the benefits in real people's stories. (We have changed the names of the people in the stories to protect their identity and security; many of them serve in places where it is not safe to share the Gospel.) We do not want to weigh you down with burdensome doctrine but will introduce you to life-changing truths that will refresh and transform your life. We want to help you understand and grasp more of the Gospel in practical, everyday terms.

My wife is a real-estate agent and has to write and review lots of legal documents and then translate them for her clients. We call the uncommon terms normal people don't understand "legalese." Doctrines like justification and propitiation are biblical aspects of the Gospel, but many of us do not understand and grasp words like these. We have intentionally written this in a way that we hope is easy for anyone to understand, and we use stories to help you make sense of (and remember!) difficult but beautiful benefits of the Gospel. *Chosen* is broken into an introductory day and a closing day, with four weeks of devotions in between. Whether you are reading this on your own, or going through it with your church or a small group, we hope this format will really connect with and challenge you in a practical way to dive deep into the Gospel and practice preaching it to yourself each day.

THE GREATEST HABIT

We need regular reminders of all God has done for us in the Gospel, because the Gospel fuels and motivates our desire to obey God and to serve Him. When we see how much He has done—how much He has given us in His Son—we cannot help but be changed and motivated to give Him our whole lives. And even while we are weak and feeble sinners struggling to follow a perfect Savior, the Gospel reminds us how loved we are and how much God is working in us to help us follow Him.

Author Jerry Bridges said, "The greatest habit any Christian can have is to preach the gospel to their own heart every day."

There is no greater need in your Christian life than regularly reminding your own heart of the truth of the Gospel.

—Matt Brown and Ryan Skoog

1

WE HAVE A BRIGHT FUTURE IN JESUS CHRIST

*The Spirit of the Lord is on me, because he has
anointed me to proclaim good news
to the poor. He has sent me to proclaim
freedom for the prisoners.*

—Luke 4:18

My friend Mr. Bai was a professor at Beijing University, known as "the Harvard of China." He once famously lay down in front of the iron gates at the entrance of the school to prevent students from leaving the campus to join a potentially dangerous protest. Mr. Bai knew the danger and told the students they would have to dishonor him and step over his body to join the protest. Most of the students stayed back. The protests that night sparked the massacre of Tiananmen Square. Mr. Bai's heroics saved scores of students' lives.

However, he made a joke in class about the Communist party to a group of students. One of those students reported Mr. Bai's joke to the police. The next day officers burst into Mr. Bai's office and brought him to a remote, cold Communist prison—without warning, without a trial.

He woke up that morning as a professor chairing one of the most prestigious academic positions in the world. By nightfall, he was behind bars in prison. Chinese prisons at this time were some of the worst places on earth—horrible lairs of disease, torture, and death. Mr. Bai quickly plunged into depression and despair. His depression led to thoughts of suicide over the course of weeks. One afternoon, in a cloud of sadness, he brought himself to the window of his eighth-story prison cell. The Chinese did not put windows in the higher floors of prison cells. If a prisoner decided to throw himself to his death, it was not a problem.

Mr. Bai's heart raced as he looked out and thought of jumping. And then it happened. He heard a small voice say, "Don't go. Don't go. Don't go." He sat down in the middle of his cell, desperate.

There on the hard concrete floor, strange memories flooded his mind. A friend of his, a foreign professor who was a Christian, had shared the Gospel with him. This friend had walked him through the story of Christ—how He took the burden of our sins on the cross and in turn offered forgiveness and a new life starting now in this world and going on forever in heaven.

Mr. Bai prayed, "Jesus, if You are real, please bring me this forgiveness and peace my friend told me You promised. In turn, I will offer my life and service to You."

He looked up and, as he tells the story now, "The sky was never bluer, the sun was never brighter through the open hole of a window, and I had joy rise up inside of my heart like I have never felt before."

This distinguished professor threw all of his reservations away and shouted out, "I have bright future in Jesus Christ!" There in the prison cell he said it again, this time louder: "I have bright future in Jesus Christ!" The guards heard him this time and cruelly told him to be quiet. But his joy could not be contained. He kept shouting it over and over until they came into the cell and beat him.

A person in a prison freed by believing the Gospel of Jesus is freer than any person outside of prison without the Gospel.

Mr. Bai was eventually released and started several orphanages in the interior of China, caring for the poor and leading many to Christ. He had a bright future in

Jesus Christ. To this day his joy is infectious when you meet him. And he will tell you the joy he had in prison is the same he has to this day.

Every person feels at times they are in a prison of their own making—trapped by thoughts, habits, actions, and a nagging past that will not let them go.

The Gospel teaches us that the worst of all prisons is the one we make for ourselves. The cells of this prison are barred with our insecurities, with the deep awareness that something is not right inside us, that something is deeply broken. We carry this with us like chains around our necks. It is the human condition.

This will only change if something drastic happens.

The Gospel is the most drastic of measures. It's a bloody cross. It's the death of God Himself for our sake. It's the utter smashing defeat of death itself in a glorious resurrection to show God's love and power throughout all eternity.

What would happen if you woke up and reminded yourself of the Gospel every day? It would be Easter every morning. How different would your life be? How much more joyful, grateful, secure, and loved would you be?

Scripture reminds us that we must pay close attention to what we have heard, especially when it comes to the Gospel (Hebrews 2:1). The most important sermon you will ever preach is the one you preach to your own heart, daily reminding your heart, "I have a bright future in Jesus Christ."

Jesus, every day is a battle to realize the brightness of Your Gospel in the midst of the darkness of this world. Lift my eyes to see just how bright Your light is today.

—Ryan Skoog

WEEK 1
THE GOSPEL

TRAINING YOUR SOUL

Bless the LORD, *O my soul, and all that is within me, bless his holy name!*

—Psalm 103:1 (ESV)

"These guys respond to challenge, so get in their faces and challenge them!"

NFL chaplain Terry Boynton got in my face and challenged me before I spoke to a roomful of professional football players. Trying to challenge athletes who each weigh in at more than three hundred pounds of lean muscle can intimidate anyone. What would you say?

I challenged them to start training their souls with the same intensity that they train their bodies.

One of the primary ways we train our souls to love God is by preaching the Gospel to our souls. The more your soul sees the cross of Jesus, the more gratefulness and adoration will well up within you. Humans are conditioned to respond that way to sacrifice. And it would be difficult to imagine a greater sacrifice than what Jesus did.

If you travel the world, one phrase that almost universally resonates—across every kind of culture—is the familiar line from Psalm 103: "Bless the LORD, O my soul" (verse 1, ESV).

Break this phrase down. David is training his soul by preaching to it. David told his soul how to feel *and* how to respond to the Gospel: *Soul, bless God, whether you want to or not.* He was not just singing a pretty line; he was talking to himself, challenging his soul to step up. Scripture describes this habit, saying, "David strengthened himself in the LORD" (1 Samuel 30:6, ESV).

It's truly a lost art of Christianity, a beautiful discipline. Instead of taking cues from your current mood, the fickle culture, the people around you, or, even more tragically, from social media, look your soul in the eyes and tell it to look to the cross, to the resurrection. Command your soul to drink in the kindness of Christ, whose bruised and splintered shoulders carried the weight of your sin.

Sometimes you must literally force your soul to look. John the Baptist called out to the cosmos, "Behold!" or "You must look!" He said, "Look, the Lamb of God, who takes away the sin of the world!" (John 1:29). This is a daily command. We *must* look! Look to the cross where Jesus suffered incredibly for a sin He never committed so that you could rejoice greatly in righteousness you never deserved.

Years ago, I started a habit not to let a day go by that I don't thank Jesus for the cross. It took years to do it consistently. Now I am praying for the Holy Spirit to help me not go half a day without stopping and thanking Christ for the cross. Few habits have transformed my life more than this simple one.

The Gospel becomes daily food for our souls, strengthening our hearts. It's much harder to complain, feel sorry for ourselves, or be filled with anxiety when our souls see the blood running down the thorn-pierced face of Christ. Gratefulness naturally builds up in our hearts when we do this throughout the day. Sometimes it feels like grateful praise is exploding in my heart, making me weak in the knees.

As one hymn says, "It makes me tremble, tremble, tremble . . ."

And when I tremble in holy reverence at the foot of the cross in the morning, I don't tremble so much at the challenges I face throughout the day.

Jesus, help me not go a single day without thanking You for the cross and remembering the power of Your resurrection.

—Ryan Skoog

3

THE CORE OF THE GOSPEL

For what I received I passed on to you as of
first importance: that Christ died for
our sins according to the Scriptures, that he
was buried, that he was raised on
the third day according to the Scriptures.
—1 Corinthians 15:3–4

I was in a small souvenir shop in a foreign country when an angry man confronted me: "You are an American. I will not even shake your hand. I don't like Americans." I sometimes wonder why he felt the need to tell me he would not shake my hand. I never asked.

He then asked, "Why are you here?" He asked, so I told him.

I shared that we were in his country to tell people about Jesus.

He looked at me and said, "Who is Jesus? I have never heard that name." Think about that. He had never even heard His name. Well, he asked, so I told him.

He listened as I shared the story of God's love in sending Christ, purchasing the forgiveness for our sins, and offering the eternal life He planned for us. The more I shared about Jesus, the more he seemed to soften.

He then looked at me and said, "I have never heard this before. This is . . . Well, I don't know what to say. But I will shake your hand. Thank you."

The story still pierces people's hearts.

I've started several travel technology companies that help thousands of churches and ministries with airfare and travel insurance for their mission trips. If you dive into the tech world, you'll find at the core of practically every computer—whether it's a mainframe computer running our power grid, a website server, or a pocket calculator—is a silicon chip. This chip is the core of all computers in all countries of the world.

The Gospel is the core "chip" powering true Christianity in all of its forms around the globe: the Chinese house church, the Christian Business Leader gatherings in Africa, a missionary in a war zone helping refugees, an aftercare center for children freed from slavery, the ornate Greek Orthodox monasteries, a rural Christian school, the inner-city discipleship and mentoring program, the megachurch celebration service, the Christian hospital in India. The Gospel is what we all share in common.

Scripture teaches us to guard the line of what is and is not the Gospel. Many fights will break out and unnecessarily escalate over issues that are not the Gospel until we know what it is . . . and what it is not. Thankfully, Scripture teaches us what the "chip" is:

> *I want to remind you of the gospel I preached to you, which you received and on which you have taken your stand. By this gospel you are saved, if you hold firmly to the word I preached to you. Otherwise, you have believed in vain. For what I received I passed on to you as of first importance: that Christ died for our sins according to the Scriptures, that he was buried, that he was raised on the third day according to the Scriptures. (1 Corinthians 15:1–4)*

This is the core. I deserve death because of my sin. Jesus died instead of me. But death has lost; Jesus is alive. The Bible tells me so.

The sacrificial death of Christ and His powerful resurrection are the core truth, the foundation of all

Christianity—the Gospel. At times it seems too simple. Scripture recognizes this tension and addresses it for us:

We preach Christ crucified: a stumbling block to Jews and foolishness to Gentiles, but to those whom God has called, both Jews and Greeks, Christ the power of God and the wisdom of God. (1 Corinthians 1:23–24)

The Gospel is like the ocean; it is so simple even a small child can wade into its waters. Yet if you keep walking, you will find a depth beyond your imagination. If you keep exploring the Gospel, you will find a mystery that confounds even the angels, who "long to look into these things" (1 Peter 1:12).

Dear Jesus, help me to see how Your death and resurrection have changed absolutely everything, both in my life and for all of time.

—Ryan Skoog

THE WOUNDS

"He himself bore our sins" in his body on the cross, so that we might die to sins and live for righteousness; "by his wounds you have been healed."

—1 Peter 2:24

"Christianity is not safe here; we must be careful," he told us as we quietly made our way out into the dark of midnight. Our anxious guide continually looked left and right as we walked along dark alleys without streetlights. We were off to meet an underground church leader, someone who oversaw tens of thousands of believers in house churches scattered throughout the country.

We packed into a small room, in a smelly building, to hear a saint tell his story.

He was arrested for sharing the Gospel of Jesus and sent to a horrible prison work camp. One meal per day, fourteen hours of labor—and that was a good day.

One night, the guard brought him in front of the entire assembly of prisoners. He commanded him to reject Christ or face a beating with a stick. He responded, "How could I ever reject my Jesus, when He has done so much for me?"

They beat him in front of the entire prison.

The next night, before his wounds could heal, the guards confronted him again. And he gave the same response. And they beat him again.

This went on for a hundred days in a row. His courage and resolve started converting so many of the prisoners to Christ that they stopped the torturous spectacle to prevent the entire prison from becoming Christians.

This is the conviction of someone who has truly understood not only what Christ suffered, but what Christ suffered *specifically for him*. Even decades later in this sweaty small room, he teared up at the mere mention of the cross of Christ, as if he were there personally witnessing the crucifixion. I saw more joy in his eyes than I can remember seeing in anyone's. I had met someone who was truly and deeply grateful for the wounds of Christ.

Later I read about hematidrosis, a medical condition where you are under so much stress that your capillaries burst near your sweat glands and you sweat blood. Dr. Alexander Metherell believes Christ experienced hematidrosis the night before He was beaten and crucified. One effect of hematidrosis is your skin becomes far more sensitive for the next few days. He believes when Christ was whipped, beaten, and nailed to a splintered cross, His skin would have been vastly more sensitive and the pain much more intense.[1]

There are no words to describe this kind of love. We've been trying in a thousand songs for thousands of years—and we've only just begun.

I really believe gratefulness is the spring of human joy. In our family we try not to say the words *happy* and *unhappy* but instead use the words *grateful* and *ungrateful*.

It's hard for me to think of something fostering more gratefulness than the wounds of Christ. The scars won't go away, you know. His hands are pierced for all eternity, marking His love for us. They are the most beautiful scars.

> *Thank You, Jesus, for loving us so much that You endured beatings and torture for our sake. There are no words, only gratefulness.*
>
> —Ryan Skoog

THE CROSS

*Surely he took up our pain and bore our suffering,
yet we considered him punished by God,
stricken by him, and afflicted. But he was pierced
for our transgressions, he was crushed for our
iniquities; the punishment that brought us peace
was on him, and by his wounds we are healed.*

—Isaiah 53:4–5

Friedrich Nietzsche infamously shocked the world with the words "God is dead."

He was half right.

God died . . . and with Him, my sin and your sin— our pride and selfishness, our addictions and insecurities, and the power of evil over us—died as well.

For many, the death of God is hidden in mystery. Why would He ever do this? Even Scripture calls the Gospel a "mystery" (Romans 16:25; Ephesians 3:6; Ephesians 6:19; Colossians 1:26).

The Bible gives a forest of reasons, the center of which is "in order that in the coming ages he might show the incomparable riches of his grace, expressed in his kindness to us in Christ Jesus" (Ephesians 2:7). We will never, ever stop praising Jesus for the cross—for ten thousand years, and then ten thousand more.

When I was a child, my mother placed a small sign on the wall in my room. It said, "I asked the Lord how much He loved me. He looked at me and said, 'This much,' and stretched out His arms as wide as He could . . . and died." A concrete display of the greatness of God's love is His personal sacrifice for the very people who betrayed Him.

But Christ did not die alone on the cross.

Scripture teaches us Jesus took evil itself—each of our pasts, and even the wrath of God itself—in His mortal body when He was crucified. The apostle Paul said, "For we know that our old self was crucified with him so that the body ruled by sin might be done away with, that we should no longer be slaves to sin" (Romans 6:6).

This difficult-to-grasp aspect of the Gospel often becomes the sweetest when we finally understand it. The death of Christ is the death of our regrets and sins.

This is why centuries of Christian songs have focused on the cross of Christ. Perhaps one of the most famous declares: "When I survey the wondrous cross on which the Prince of glory died . . . love so amazing, so divine, demands my soul, my life, my all."

Take time to look at the cross. To survey it. Or in other words, to look at it from every angle imaginable. It takes study and meditation and maybe even a few tears to grasp even a small part of the depths of God's love on the cross.

The more we stare at love crucified, the easier it becomes to surrender all of our life. Or as one missionary, C. T. Studd, said, "If Jesus Christ be God and died for me, then no sacrifice can be too great for me to make for Him."

One night I was praying desperately after experiencing one of the biggest emotional pains of my life. I told Jesus, "This feels like a knife in my heart." Then it happened. I closed my eyes and saw a picture of Jesus taking the knife, removing it from my heart, and then plunging it into His own. And I heard a voice in my heart say, "This is what I do for you; I take it for you."

I cried even more, but these were tears of grateful awe at the depth of Jesus's love. The pain I felt that night was not a big deal compared with how others have suffered in history, but Christ came to me personally and took it all the same.

There is a poem in Scripture that shares this idea. It's the very heart of the Gospel: "Surely he took up our pain and bore our suffering. . . . He was pierced for our transgressions, he was crushed for our iniquities; the punishment that brought us peace was on him, and by his wounds we are healed" (Isaiah 53:4–5). Christ bore both our sin and the painful effects of sin on the cross. The prophet Isaiah told us Christ bore our "pain" and "suffering" at the same time He bore our "transgressions" and "iniquities."

Look no further than the cross if you want to see the love of God on full display for the universe.

> *Jesus, the cross is the center of all time; help it to become the center of my life and the lens through which I see everything.*
>
> —Ryan Skoog

THE DEATH

*For our sake [God] made him to be sin . . .so that
in him we might become the righteousness of God.*

—2 Corinthians 5:21 (ESV)

It's not every day a former genocidal mass murderer sits in your office.

Colonel Hallounn was a leader in the army of a ruling dictator of a rogue, sanctioned nation. He had orders to commit the systematic genocide of a minority people group. He would shoot minorities with a machine gun. Sometimes they would fight back. There's still shrapnel in his body from these fights.

One night, the colonel had a dream. Jesus appeared to him and told him to stop killing and to "follow Me." Alarmed by the dream, he sought out a Christian and started following this Jesus. He discovered the great truth of the Gospel—that God would forgive even him, even after he murdered crowds of people simply because of their race.

Together with friends in college, I founded a nonprofit called Venture.org, which helps thousands of people in the United States do *tough things*, like run, hike, and bike, to raise funds to help local leaders bring the Gospel to thousands of people in *tough places*. Places like Colonel Hallounn's country. Today we partner with the colonel to feed seven thousand war refugee children every single day in camps all over his country. The colonel now feeds the very people he used to shoot before he met Jesus.

The colonel still has shrapnel in his body. I guess it serves as a daily reminder of what God saved him from.

Likewise, Jesus still has scars from saving us. Jesus became sin, and sin had to die.

When Jesus took our place, it meant He had to *become* a self-righteous hypocrite, a thief, a liar, an alcoholic, a porn addict, even a mass murderer. He had to die because He took our place. And Jesus became the very worst of us. Jesus took the punishment, and we got His inheritance. It is the most unjust moment in history. It's not fair. And yet through one unfair exchange, we are made new and given everything.

Paul wrote, "For our sake [God] made him to be sin . . . so that in him we might become the righteousness of God" (2 Corinthians 5:21, ESV).

This is why God rejected Christ on the cross. Jesus took the rejection we deserved. God turned His face away from Christ so He would never have to turn His face away from us.

J. R. R. Tolkien wrote *The Lord of the Rings* trilogy, the best-selling book series of all time behind the Bible. He said his inspiration for writing one of the most beloved and treasured stories was the cross. He said it was a small event, with one Person making one sacrificial gesture, that changed the entire course of eternity.

Being a master of language, Tolkien made up his own English word for this event, a *eucatastrophe*: "the sudden happy turn in a story which pierces you with a joy that brings tears, a sudden and miraculous grace."[2] The cross is your *eucatastrophe*, a small event that happened in an insignificant part of the world that pierces your heart and changes the entire course of your life, and those whom your life touches, and the lives *those* people touch, and on and on for eternity.

Jesus, please remind me daily of how Your death changes the darkest parts of my story into a beautiful epic of grace.

—Ryan Skoog

THE EMPTY TOMB

Then Simon Peter came along behind him
and went straight into the tomb.

—John 20:6

If you remind yourself of the death and resurrection of Jesus each day—living as if every day is Easter morning—you can live every day without regret.

Carnegie Mellon University did a study of the most common emotions humans experience. Right after love, the second most common human emotion—across all races, cultures, countries—is regret. The study identified five common regrets people experience: romance, family, education, career, and finance.[3]

When Henry David Thoreau wrote, "The mass of men lead lives of quiet desperation," I believe he was observing the desperation of regret. We often walk around with regret like a heavy weight around our necks, pulling our vision away from the stars in the heavens down to the mud and dust of the earth.

Psychologists diagnose and document the effects of regret on the body, mind, and emotions. Phobias, disorders, domestic violence, substance abuse, rage, depression, and anxiety all can be traced back to *regret*. The Gospel is not just a nice addition to your life; the cross plunges deep into the source of many of these human maladies of the heart and kills these powerful roots of regret.

The other day I was moving heavy furniture into our house and my children kept trying to talk to me. With a grunt I told them, "Can't talk . . . heavy load." Many of us feel we cannot talk to God because we, too, are carrying such heavy loads of regret.

Peter walked around with an incalculable amount of regret. His best friend Jesus died, and the last thing Peter did before his friend died was betray Him. There was no way to say "sorry." There was nothing Peter could do to go back to that moment and make things right. He was left in the desperation of regret.

Peter's first encounter of the resurrection was not meeting Jesus. Before he saw Him, he saw an empty tomb. We don't know if anyone else went into the tomb, but we know Peter did. Maybe God let Peter be the first because of all the regret he was carrying.

When we preach the Gospel to ourselves, we step back into the empty tomb. I like to picture throwing my regrets in the tomb and waking up the next morning to find it empty.

If Jesus never left the tomb, we would still carry our regrets everywhere we go. Our hope would have died with Him. But because He rose, we can leave behind everything we're ashamed of. We can enjoy the forgiveness and freedom of an empty tomb.

Because of the cross, when you look back to your moments of regret, you will find only an empty room. Regrets vanish; the tomb is empty.

Imagine what life could be like if you knew you were totally, completely forgiven from everything and made whole.

Jesus, help my heart to believe You when You say I can be free of regrets because You took them all on the cross.

—Ryan Skoog

THE RESURRECTION

And if Christ has not been raised, your faith is futile; you are still in your sins.

—1 Corinthians 15:17

A local church once took a mission trip to build a church in a remote village in Russia. They were building the house of worship from the stones of an abandoned Russian prison. What a powerful scene!

Careful attention was taken to preserve the stones. While removing one of the large stones, they discovered a hollowed-out stone with a canister in it; inside the canister was a hastily written note: "We are a group of Christians being forced by Communists to take the stones of our church and build a prison where we will stay until we die. Our prayer is one day these stones would once again be used to build a church."

Prison stones turned into a place of worship. Tombstones rolled away. Death completely swallowed up in victory. Resurrection.

When Christ rose from the dead, He chose to reveal Himself first to Mary Magdalene. In those days, the testimony of a woman would not even hold up in court. But Jesus picked a poor minority woman as His first witness, showing the world a minority woman with the greatest news in the world can subvert the largest, most dominant empire in the history of humankind. And now today, God's kingdom is growing by the thousands every day, men and women committing their lives to Christ, while the Roman kingdom lies in ruins.

The Gospel story is a story of ordinary people witnessing and experiencing the extraordinary power of the resurrection. Whenever you feel poor and powerless, the resurrected Christ stands ready to reveal His power through you. All of the areas of your life that feel insignificant are exactly where Christ is looking to do another resurrection miracle.

Christ did His greatest miracles among the most ordinary people, in the most insignificant towns, at the most ordinary times. The majority of miracles were not done in the temple of Jerusalem but on the outskirts of tiny villages. If you are in an unremarkable place, you just might be in the perfect environment for the resurrection power of God to break out.

When you start sharing the Gospel with your own heart every day, you will start seeing resurrection in the most normal and average of days, places, and people.

Or as Wendell Berry reminded us in his poem "Manifesto: The Mad Farmer Liberation Front," resurrection is a daily practice.

> *So, friends, every day do something*
> *that won't compute. Love the Lord. . . .*
> *Ask the questions that have no answers. . . .*
> *Practice resurrection.*[4]

Jesus, help me to live every day practicing Your resurrection in my thoughts, decisions, and interactions.

—Ryan Skoog

WEEK 2

THE GOSPEL
CHANGES OUR PAST

BLESSED

All praise to God, the Father of our Lord Jesus
Christ, who has blessed us with every
spiritual blessing in the heavenly realms
because we are united with Christ.

—Ephesians 1:3 (NLT)

The cross and the resurrection change everything.
They change our past, present, and future. For the next
three weeks you will be walking through the new past
that has been changed forever, the new present reality
we live in, and the new future we can look forward
to—all because of the Gospel.

The apostle Paul wrote a letter to the churches
in Ephesus; they were exploding with growth at the
time. He launched with a long run-on sentence; some
scholars believe this is the longest run-on sentence
in the entire New Testament. It's as if he took a deep
breath and virtually erupted about how the Gospel

has changed the entire cosmos—and each of our lives in the process.

Every blessing included is intentionally listed in the past tense. We cannot earn these blessings; we already have them if we've become a Christian—all of us. You have been forgiven, you have been chosen, you have been redeemed *already*. The gift has already been given. This week we will walk through this run-on sentence and look in order at each of the aspects of our past that have been changed forever because of the Gospel. For today, remind yourself that you have been *blessed*.

I nearly dropped the book when I read David Bentley Hart's translation of the word *blessed* in the Bible. The famous scholar talks about how *blessed* has lost its meaning in our culture: it is used more or less as "lucky" or "fortunate." Instead, Hart argues the real meaning would be much closer to our word *blissful* or a state of enraptured happiness.

This is what God has done: He has given every eternal blessing imaginable to us to the point that we are full of bliss, or bliss-full.

Our daily choice, our daily fight, our daily trial is whether or not to remember, realize, and live in this reality. And it is not based upon circumstances. It's really not. My friend Meisha taught me this in a way I won't ever forget.

Meisha was a refugee in a war-torn country. His village and all he had ever known were destroyed by an oppressive army, and he was forced to be a porter, carrying the supplies of a soldier through a rainy jungle while staring down the barrel of a gun—much like in Jesus's day when a Roman soldier forced a person to carry his gear for a mile.

Then one day a soldier forced Meisha at gunpoint to dismantle a land mine. The mine exploded, and Meisha lost both hands and both eyes in an instant. They left him there, thinking he was dead, but he did not die.

Several years ago, someone shared with him the story of the suffering Savior. He identified with a God who knew his pain. His life was gloriously transformed.

Meisha is so blissfully excited about the Gospel that he has people lead him from refugee camp to refugee camp so that he can share the Gospel with those who have not heard about Jesus. Meisha's joy is infectious. He is far happier than most people who can see, have both hands, and don't live in survival poverty in a refugee camp. His joy springs from his gratitude for the cross. Meisha knows in a short time he will be with Christ forever.

Meisha models this by spilling out Gospel bliss in the middle of a refugee camp. He embodies the writings of the apostle Paul, who said, "Our light and momentary troubles are achieving for us an eternal glory that far outweighs them all" (2 Corinthians 4:17).

Jesus, thank You for blessing me beyond my imagination through Your sacrifice. Please open my eyes to see what You have already given me.
—Ryan Skoog

CHOSEN

*For he chose us in him before
the creation of the world.*

—Ephesians 1:4

My friend Albert grew up in a poor village in a country where the Gospel is outlawed. As a teenager, he found the opportunity to travel to another town and go to school where a Christian missionary taught English. The missionary shared the Bible in his home in secret.

Albert learned the stories of Jesus from this teacher but was not sure if he believed them.

When he went back home to his village, there was a lack of food. With a hungry belly, Albert took to the mountains to fish. After fishing for quite some time without catching anything, Albert remembered the story of Peter throwing his nets on the other side of the boat. He set down his fishing pole, bowed to his knees in the rocks along the banks of the river, and prayed, "Jesus, if You are real like my teacher told me, help me catch fish like You helped the disciples. I am hungry."

He dropped in his line and immediately started catching fish after fish! He loaded his basket with fish and went back to his village to tell everyone about this fishing spot. People from the town went to the same spot and did not catch anything. This miracle revealed the risen Christ to Albert, and he has been a changed man for thirty years now. He runs a successful business, which he uses to lead people to Jesus in a country hostile to the Gospel.

Albert grew up thinking he was nothing. Too poor, too uneducated, too unremarkable and ordinary to matter to anyone, much less to God. But God had already chosen Albert before the creation of the world. And you can be in the remote wilderness alone by a river, and the love of God will chase you and find you.

There are not many mentions of the universe *before* creation in Scripture, which makes the fact that "he chose us in him before the creation of the world" so unique and powerful.

If God chose you before creation, then nothing in creation can change it—not even "death nor life, neither angels nor demons, neither the present nor the future, nor any powers, neither height nor depth, nor anything else in all creation" (Romans 8:38–39).

And God pursues those whom He's chosen. Psalm 23 ends with a unique insight into our God who pursues us: "Surely goodness and mercy shall follow me all the days of my life, and I shall dwell in the house of the LORD forever" (verse 6, ESV).

It gets exciting when you realize the word for "follow me" could be translated "chase after me like a hunter." God's love takes on a whole new meaning. "Goodness and mercy shall hunt me down all the days of my life."

The resurrection joy of Christ has a way of chasing us no matter where we go in the world. God, the great cosmic hunter, found my friend Albert by a wilderness river—alone, hungry, poor, and hopeless.

God found you as well. And His love is chasing you today. When you stop and remind yourself of the love of God on the cross and the power of God in the resurrection, you will find yourself in the wide nets of His love.

Jesus, thank You for choosing me for salvation before the world was even created. Help me to not look for validation anywhere else or in anyone else.

—Ryan Skoog

LOVED

In love he predestined us for adoption to sonship through Jesus Christ, in accordance with his pleasure and will—to the praise of his glorious grace, which he has freely given us in the One he loves.

—Ephesians 1:4–6

D. L. Moody was a prominent nineteenth-century minister who worked in Chicago and later in Massachusetts. His son-in-law wrote down a story of how grasping the great love of God changed Moody and his ministry forever.

Moody made several trips throughout his life to England and Ireland, where God used him in significant ways. During his first visit to Ireland, a young preacher by the name of Harry Moorehouse approached Moody and essentially invited himself to preach at Moody's church in Chicago. Moody was surprised at

Moorehouse's candor and self-invitation, especially given the fact that Moorehouse looked so young. Moody privately referred to him as a "beardless boy; didn't look as if he was more than seventeen." Moody did not think it was possible he could preach well.

Moorehouse persisted, even making the trip by boat to the United States without any real invitation from Moody. Moody tried to ward him off, but Moorehouse's resilience won the day as he made his way to Chicago, informing Moody of his arrival to the U.S. by letter.

Moorehouse began the first of seven days of services preaching from John 3:16—"God so loved the world, that he gave his only begotten Son, that whosoever believeth in him should not perish, but have everlasting life" (KJV).

The second, third, fourth, fifth, sixth, and finally even the seventh night, his sermons were from the same verse—about how God so loves the world.

That first message was revelatory for Moody. In his own words,

> *He preached a most extraordinary sermon from that verse. He did not divide the text into 'secondly' and 'thirdly' and 'fourthly'—he just took it as a whole, and then went through the Bible,*

from Genesis to Revelation, to prove that in all
ages God loved the world. . . .

I never knew up to that time that God loved
us so much. This heart of mine began to thaw out,
and I could not keep back the tears. It was like
news from a far country. I just drank it in. . . .

He could turn to almost any part of the
Bible, and prove it. . . .

He just beat it down into our hearts, and I
have never doubted it since.

I used to preach that God was behind the
sinner with a double-edged sword, ready to hew
him down. I have got done with that. I preach
now that God is behind the sinner with love,
and he is running away from the God of love.

On the final night, Moorehouse walked up to
preach, and he said,

My friends, I have been hunting all day for a
new text, but I cannot find one as good as the
old one; so we will go back to [John 3:16]. . . .

My friends, for a whole week I have been
trying to tell you how much God loves you, but
I cannot do it with this poor stammering tongue.
If I could borrow Jacob's ladder, and climb up

into heaven, and ask Gabriel, who stands in
the presence of the Almighty, if he could tell me
how much love the Father has for the world, all
he could say would be: "God so loved the world,
that he gave his only begotten Son, that whoso-
ever believeth in him should not perish, but have
everlasting life."[5]

The apostle Paul told us, "In love he predestined us for adoption to sonship through Jesus Christ, in accordance with his pleasure and will" (Ephesians 1:4–5).

The Gospel is possible because of God's great love. Jesus fundamentally changes our perspective about who God is by showing us our good, good Father, who "in love" adopts us as children.

It's vital that we consider God's love for us. Paul broke into a prayer about this in the middle of Ephesians 3:

Christ will make his home in your hearts as
you trust in him. Your roots will grow down
into God's love and keep you strong. And may
you have the power to understand, as all God's
people should, how wide, how long, how high,
and how deep his love is. May you experience
the love of Christ, though it is too great to

understand fully. Then you will be made com-
plete with all the fullness of life and power that
comes from God. (verses 17–19, NLT)

Paul actually said that completeness in our faith comes from contemplating and experiencing God's great love for us. He said it is too great to understand fully, but we should spend our lives trying to grasp how wide, long, high, and deep His love is. He said we should try to grasp it but then told us we will never be able to fully. It is a love too great for words.

How do you begin to try to describe this great love of God? If you are a parent, think of your love for your child the day they were born. You can't explain it or describe it, but your heart explodes with great love.

I remember when our children were born. The very moment they were born and I held them in my arms, my heart exploded with a love too great for words. As our children grow older and go through the phases of childhood, my love never wanes. They can be a screaming toddler, and while that can be exhausting at times, my love for them is overwhelming and too impossibly great to explain. That is a tiny fraction of the love God has for us.

Jesus loves you more in a moment than anyone ever could in a lifetime.

Jesus didn't just say He loves you; He showed it in the most dramatic fashion possible. He gave His life for you on the cross to prove His love for you.

God knows the worst about you; nevertheless, He is the one who loves you the most.

Because of the Gospel, one of the names God gives us is "beloved." *Be loved.* It's actually a command to let God love us.

But we easily replace "Be Loved" with another name based on how good we think we are: "Be Better," "Be Stronger," "Be More Like Someone Else," "Be More Influential." Instead, God calls to us to just be: loved by Him.

The more we allow our hearts to humbly receive the love of God, the stronger and holier and better we naturally become as a result of being loved unconditionally.

Jesus, help me realize how high and wide and long and deep Your love is for me and everyone I meet today.

—Matt Brown

ADOPTED

*For all who are led by the Spirit of God are sons
of God. For you did not receive the spirit of
slavery to fall back into fear, but you have
received the Spirit of adoption as sons, by whom
we cry, "Abba! Father!" The Spirit himself bears
witness with our spirit that we are children
of God, and if children, then heirs—heirs of God
and fellow heirs with Christ.*

—Romans 8:14–17 (ESV)

I was raised in Minnesota, a state full of Scandinavian pacifists known for being "nice." If you get pulled over by the police, "Minnesota nice" culture says you should thank them for giving you a ticket. Because the worst thing you could ever do is not be nice.

In a dusty village in Nepal near the shadows of Mount Everest, my "Minnesota nice" quickly transformed into something like "New York rage." The village was not like other small impoverished villages. Close to 80 percent of the girls were destined to be sold into brothels because they were the lowest subgroup of the lowest caste in the country.

It was here we met Landana, the most beautiful ten-year-old girl. Her father had agreed to sell her to an Indian brothel where she would be raped dozens of times each day.

Her mother couldn't bear the thought and tried to prevent her husband from selling her precious girl. But he would not have it. He started beating his wife because she did not want to sell their girl.

When we found this out, I fought this sudden urge inside to find this man and hurt him. I feel embarrassed as I write this, but I cannot say it any other way than I wanted to assault him.

We acted quickly with local social workers, law enforcement, and our pastor partner. We got Landana to a safe house where girls like her are kept safe, warm, fed, and loved. Our nonprofit Venture.org supports 680 girls who have been rescued from brothels and slavery in Nepal. They stay in safe houses where they get an education and hear about the love of Jesus.

I never met Landana's father. I was glad I didn't.

Landana heard the Gospel. She heard how through Jesus we are adopted into God's family.

This is the most powerful part of the Gospel for most Hindus. For them, family caste is everything. It is your identity. It is your destiny. It is your last name. It defines you more than gender, culture, color, or neighborhood. Landana's caste meant she was doomed to be lower than a dog—used, sold, and abused. Hinduism teaches that in a past life she must have racked up a serious number of sins for Karma to punish her and send her back to earth as a Badi girl. What's worse is that even her own people do not help her because they do not want to prevent Karma from punishing her. As a result, Badi girls are some of the most trafficked people per capita on the planet.

When sharing the Gospel with another Badi girl, I told her, "The Gospel teaches your last name is no longer Badi. It's like your name is no longer Jarla Badi; it is Jarla 'Christ' because you are in His family, you are in His caste now." She lit up and looked at me with eyes of possibility and hope. "Can this be true?" she asked. "Yes, Jarla!" It is the truest truth in all the world.

The cross is the event that allows us to be adopted into Christ's family. The modern mind looks at

Christianity and wonders, "Why blood? How can you sing about blood?" But those who have been bought with the blood of Christ know that we now share a bond that goes much deeper than our bloodlines here on earth.

Landana gladly joined the family of God, leaving behind the shame of her family, her caste, her bloodline. Jesus is not just offering a fresh start of forgiveness; He is inviting us into a new family and a new destiny. And this is why Christians love to think about the blood of Christ.

For Landana, God became her father, and His love is the opposite of a father willing to sell his little girl. It is a God who was willing to sell Himself for thirty pieces of silver to save His little girl.

A year later we visited Landana, and she was so different. So much stronger. She was a young leader, helping other girls learn and grow.

We have a new family identity, a new family crest, a new estate, new brothers and sisters, a new last name. This is beautiful to someone who grew up being told her family line was the lowest on earth. But it is equally beautiful to those who bring their family shame to the cross and watch it melt away. With joy you can say, "My old family does not define me, my new family does!"

This is how Scripture describes it:

> For all who are led by the Spirit of God are sons
> of God. For you did not receive the spirit of slav-
> ery to fall back into fear, but you have received
> the Spirit of adoption as sons, by whom we cry,
> "Abba! Father!" The Spirit himself bears witness
> with our spirit that we are children of God, and
> if children, then heirs—heirs of God and fellow
> heirs with Christ. (Romans 8:14–17, ESV)

If you listen, the Holy Spirit is whispering daily, "You have a new Father, a new family."

This Gospel goes beyond purging our past of its sin; it purges our entire ancestry, lineage, extended family of its shame. You are not primarily a part of an earthly family anymore; you have joined a heavenly family. The blood of Jesus marks you as family for all eternity.

But the Gospel is not only for the oppressed; the Gospel is also for the oppressor.

After witnessing the transformation in Landana's life, her father, the very man I wanted to beat up, became a Christian as well. He is now my brother, in my family.

Jesus, the cross says You are my brother. Thank You, ten thousand times thank You, for inviting me into Your family.

—Ryan Skoog

REDEEMED

In him we have redemption.

—Ephesians 1:7

"That's it, I'm ending it all."

This text showed up on my phone from an unknown number on a Tuesday night at 8:00 p.m. I had just sat down on the couch after kissing my kids good night after a long day.

"I'm sorry, who is this?" I texted back.

Her name was Sarah. She realized she had texted the wrong number and apologized.

"Wait a minute . . ." I texted. "I can help."

We started texting back and forth for around half an hour. She told me her story. It was tragic. The final wound was her current abusive boyfriend breaking up with her. I kept trying to let her know about the love of Jesus and her worth to God in spite of all she felt. I told her not to base her life on the opinion of a twenty-two-year-old boy.

But I was too late.

"It's too late—I just downed an entire bottle of pills."

I begged her to tell me where she was. I told her my wife and I could come bring her to the hospital. She told me, and we rushed her to the hospital, where they immediately treated Sarah and saved her life.

Over the coming months, Sarah's eyes were slowly opened to see how valuable she is in Christ. She even ended up going to a Christian university to pursue God's plan for her life. God had redeemed her; He had taken a life deemed worthless by our world—and even by herself—and flipped it around. She was worth dying for.

When I was getting an MBA in entrepreneurship, my economics professor drilled into our heads a fundamental concept: *The value of something is determined by what someone will pay for it.* The price paid for our redemption is the blood of Jesus Christ, the Son of God. Could there be a greater price? Could anything make you worth more?

We each fight a daily battle to base our worth on the price God paid for us. We each have some other currency we use to measure our worth. We use the currency of accomplishments, family, looks, wealth, race, education, leadership ability, influence numbers, or "fill in the blank." Humans are either desperately trying to prove their worth or living in depression because they feel they do not have worth.

This is one of the more powerful effects of preaching the Gospel to your soul. You are reminding your soul of its worth in Christ by reminding yourself of the high price that was paid to redeem you.

Jesus, thank You for paying the ultimate price for my life. Help me derive my value and worth from Your sacrifice instead of any other measurement of this world.

—Ryan Skoog

FORGIVEN

In him we have . . . the forgiveness of sins, in accordance with the riches of God's grace.

—Ephesians 1:7

"Saved alone, what shall I do?"

Anna Spafford sent this tragic telegram on December 2, 1873, from Cardiff, Wales, to her husband, Horatio, a lawyer in Chicago. Her transatlantic steamboat, *Ville du Havre*, collided with another ship and sank. Anna was one of only a few survivors, but their four daughters all went down with the *Ville du Havre*.

Horatio boarded the very next available ship and made the two-week journey across the same sea that took his four daughters. These were undoubtedly the longest two weeks of his life.

With pain incalculable, Horatio started writing lyrics. In this dark hour, he reminded himself of the Gospel. And joy started welling up in his heart:

My sin, oh, the bliss of the glorious thought!
My sin, not in part but the whole,
Is nailed to the cross, and I bear it no more,
Praise the Lord, praise the Lord, O my soul!

It is well with my soul,
It is well, it is well with my soul.[6]

In the midst of tragedy, the beauty of forgiveness became a source of true joy. The cross was still beautiful on the ship that day, even to a father who had lost four daughters. The Gospel is not just a comfort to our greatest shame; it is a comfort in our darkest nights.

The secret to experiencing the joy of forgiveness is seeing the depths of your sin. It is realizing that even your good works require forgiveness because sin mars even our best works.

Understanding this changed my wife's life because it changed her relationship with God. She was called Ms. Goody Two-Shoes growing up. She had a 4.0 at school, volunteered at church, led her friends to Christ, worked toward racial reconciliation as a high schooler, never kissed a boy until she was engaged, never rebelled against her parents, teachers, or authorities. She's one of the kindest, most humble people I know. But because she seemed so good, she never realized the depth of her sin and the depth of God's forgiveness.

But sin is not only something we do; it is our broken nature.

Toward the end of his life, psychologist Sigmund Freud summarized the depths of mankind's broken state in a single phrase: *Homo homini lupus* [man is wolf to man]. It still echoes today.

Freud went on, "Who in the face of all his experience of life and of history, will have the courage to dispute this assertion?"[7] No one came forward publically. The philosophy giant Immanuel Kant agreed: "Out of the crooked timber of humanity, no straight thing was ever made."

Scripture puts it this way: "As for you, you were dead" (Ephesians 2:1).

But wait, it's worse! Scripture goes on to say that because of our sin, we also are "deserving of wrath" (Ephesians 2:3).

In short, we are not good. Not one of us. We are trolls, and our good deeds are only lipstick. Even the best of us. We all have reason to love much, because we *all* have been forgiven much.

My friend, when asked how he is doing, often says, "Better than I deserve . . ."

Is there a better feeling than being forgiven? I could smile for a week if a policeman said, "I won't give you a speeding ticket this time." The rush of peace and relief is tangible. The Gospel teaches us we have been forgiven of so much more—of *everything*, absolutely everything.

We could smile for a lifetime.

Jesus, thank You for bringing total forgiveness to my life, my past, my future. Help me to live free and forgiven and offer forgiveness to others.
—Ryan Skoog

INCLUDED

And you also were included in Christ when you heard the message of truth, the gospel of your salvation. When you believed, you were marked in him with a seal, the promised Holy Spirit.

—Ephesians 1:13

When I was young, my father had an important role at a large company. If you wanted to walk into his office, you would have to get past the front desk, then past rows of workers, past mid-level managers, and finally past his secretary. But as a ten-year-old, I could walk right past all of these people and open his door because he was my dad. Likewise, we can walk past all of the angelic hosts, saints, and powerful beings of heaven right into the throne room of the God of heaven and say, "Father."

We are His children, and He wants to be with us.

When Jesus picked His disciples, there is a curious phrase used. He picked those to "be with him" (Mark 3:14). I suggest that Jesus was less concerned about who He could delegate authority to, who would represent Him, or who would be the great leaders, and was more interested in choosing men to be with Him. Jesus said, "Abide in me" (John 15:4, ESV), meaning "live all of life with Me." It's a constant discipline to spend the simple moments of every day with Jesus, but when we stay close to Him, we will bear much fruit; it will naturally flow out of that closeness.

The Jewish historian Rabbi Yohanan ben Zakkai wrote about a time when the doors of the temple mysteriously flung open.[8] (He wrote this around forty years before the destruction of Jerusalem, right around the time of Christ's crucifixion.) The Bible teaches us that more than opening the doors, the thick veil covering the Holy of Holies in the temple was strangely ripped when Christ died. The veil was meant to separate or shield humans from God's intense and holy presence. Once and forever it was torn apart by the death of Christ.

This thick curtain is also a symbol—a picture of how we were separated from God. The Gospel gives us this beautiful picture of all the things holding us away from God being torn apart from top to bottom.

You may think, because of something in your life or past, that God's love cannot reach you. But Jesus tore it apart.

When I was in college, I used to walk around really tough neighborhoods in our city with my friend Chuck, simply praying under our breath for everyone around us. We read a book on prayer walking. It's a powerful habit. If anyone asked, we told people we were asking God to bless everyone we saw. Most people thought we were looking for drugs.

One day we came around a corner and made eye contact with a guy on the sidewalk. I said, "Hey." His response was not what we could have ever expected.

"Man, I need the Lord."

We stopped walking.

He went on: "I saw you come around the corner, and it was like a light was with you. I could just tell you were with the Lord."

I looked down to see if we were wearing anything Christian—necklace, T-shirt, anything. Nothing.

He went on: "I'm an alcoholic, and I'm done. I want out. I want to get off the streets, into rehab. Can you help?"

We piled into our rusty minivan, every college student's dream, and drove to a local Christian rehab center. We were able to check him in that very day. We checked back later and discovered he had found freedom from alcoholism.

God's presence with us is real and more tangible than we realize. Sometimes others can literally see it. You are different because of the Gospel, and the difference will only grow the longer you walk with the Lord.

Jesus, thank You for offering the greatest invitation to life through Your resurrection. Help me to accept this invitation in every part of my life today.

—Ryan Skoog

WEEK 3
THE GOSPEL
CHANGES OUR PRESENT

16

GOD IS SAVING US

For the message of the cross is foolishness
to those who are perishing, but to us who are
being saved it is the power of God.

—1 Corinthians 1:18

The Gospel is beautiful. It is the truest truth in all the world. It has spurred the greatest acts of compassion and sacrifice. It's a story that transcends any political, cultural, or racial boundaries. It resonates across history and through generations. The Gospel is not something that happened; it is happening. We are only beginning to see its beauty.

Many Christians have lost the impact of the Gospel, thinking the good news is old news. But Scripture teaches us to "pay much closer attention to what we have heard, lest we drift away from it" (Hebrews 2:1, ESV)—not because we have heard it too many times but because we have not looked into it deeply enough.

Saying, "I already know the Gospel, I've heard it all before," is like someone thinking they know what is going on in outer space because they have looked up at the night sky. Yes, you can see its beauty instantly, but it would be silly to think your glance helps you even begin to comprehend everything about the storms of Jupiter and the supernova explosions in deep space. In the same way, there are depths of beauty in the Gospel that must be explored, and to do this very act strengthens the faith of the believer like no other practice.

Christian theology never "gets past" the Gospel into deeper truths; it builds on the Gospel to grow into everything God has for us. The believer never moves beyond their need for understanding and reminding themselves about the truths contained within in the Gospel.

Looking closer at the Gospel, one example is the present-tense saving power of God.

Salvation did not happen; it is *happening* right now. We were not saved; we "are being saved" (1 Corinthians 1:18). God anchored this truth into the very name of Jesus, which means "God saves," present tense. Another way to say this is: God *is* saving you every second of every day.

I love this truth because I need it. My heart needs the saving grace of God hour by hour.

Find moments each day to remember that God *is* saving you, present tense, right now. It was finished on the cross, but it's happening with every step you take with Christ. It is God's nature, His very name, to be saving you right now.

Jesus, thank You for saving me every moment of every day; help me to practice living aware of Your saving grace moment by moment today.
—Ryan Skoog

PEACE

Peace I leave with you; my peace I give you. I do not give to you as the world gives. Do not let your hearts be troubled and do not be afraid.

—John 14:27

The turmoil in our world is not new. For thousands of years there have been wars and rumors of wars, unrest, governments being overthrown, pain, sickness, famine, death, natural disasters. This is the world we live in, and it has always been the world we live in. But through the Gospel, Jesus gives us real peace in the midst of the storms of our day.

Jesus never promised Christians an easy life. He said, "I have told you these things, so that in me you may have peace. In this world you will have trouble. But take heart! I have overcome the world" (John 16:33).

He promised us a glorious eternity, but He warned us this life would be hard. Without an eternal perspective and unusual hope in the Gospel, the pain of this life would be unbearable.

Jesus promised to give us a peace on the inside, even when there is not peace on the outside. He told us not to be troubled, anxious, or fearful, even when life is hard, challenging, or unexpected, because He is with us.

This peace that the Gospel gives us will regularly boggle our minds and the minds of the people around us. Paul wrote, "The peace of God, which transcends all understanding, will guard your hearts and your minds in Christ Jesus" (Philippians 4:7). You won't understand how you have peace like this, but you will sense it deeply, no matter what you go through.

Peace with God is the foundation for peace in every other area of our lives. We find peace with God through the Gospel, and that peace affects and shapes how we interact with and react to others.

Because of the Gospel, we now go through our days from the bedrock foundation of God's peace, and we are better able to bring this incredible peace to the world around us.

Jesus, thank You for enduring the cross to bring us peace, peace that doesn't even make sense sometimes.

—Matt Brown

PURPOSE

For it is by grace you have been saved, through faith—and this is not from yourselves, it is the gift of God—not by works, so that no one can boast. For we are God's handiwork, created in Christ Jesus to do good works, which God prepared in advance for us to do.

—Ephesians 2:8–10

Jason landed his dream job in Bristol, Connecticut—the kind of job any guy dreams of having, "working" to cover sports all day at ESPN. He worked there over the next seventeen years, working with some of the most talented broadcasters in the world. He wasn't a Christian when he first arrived, but his brother prayed fervently for him and one day told him about his hope in Jesus.

In the years after Jason was saved, he felt that although he was doing his dream job, God must have more important work for him to do in full-time minis-try. One day he was giving a tour to Tony Dungy and his assistant, and he was sharing these feelings. Dungy's assistant pulled him aside at one point and said, "You don't get it, do you? God has you right where you are supposed to be." Jason hadn't realized that God can use us right where we are, wherever we are.

But this past year, Jason sensed God truly was call-ing him away from ESPN. God was giving him a desire to do more ministry. He left his dream job for God's call, and God has been blessing him and using him in significant ways. Even the fact that someone would leave ESPN to pursue ministry has impacted a lot of people around the nation.

The apostle Paul told us that God has a purpose for all of us. He has prepared good works for each of us to do (Ephesians 2:10). We are not saved by our good works; we are saved by Christ's work on the cross. But the Gospel propels us into good works like nothing else can. We long to give our everything for God's glory. And God has prepared people for us to impact, places for us to serve, and resources for us to give.

For my friend Jason, staying in his dream job at ESPN or leaving for something else was not really the issue. For a season, God had a purpose for him to be there. That was his ministry for years—showing the love of Christ by his attitude, interactions, and conversations with coworkers. But a time came when he had a clear sense that God had a purpose for him outside that role, and he courageously left to follow God's leading. God continues to bless Jason's efforts everywhere he goes because God has prepared good works in advance for him to do.

God has a purpose for all of us, and that is to follow His leading and discover good works we can do wherever we are.

Jesus, it's because of Your love and sacrifice that I get to live Your dreams, which are much greater than mine.

—Matt Brown

SIGNIFICANCE

See what great love the Father has lavished on us, that we should be called children of God! And that is what we are! The reason the world does not know us is that it did not know him.

—1 John 3:1

When you believe in Jesus, you get something greater than any achievement, accomplishment, or title you could ever earn on this earth. You become a son or daughter of the King. The Bible calls us coheirs with Christ. Everything that is His is ours. In Him, we have far more than we could ever need or even want.

If you are greatly valued by the King of the universe, does it matter much who undervalues you here on this earth?

Our significance is no longer measured by social media "likes" or followers. Our significance is no longer measured by our relationship status, our looks, or how we dress. Our significance is no longer measured by how far we climb the ladder at our job or how much money or possessions we are able to attain. Our significance is no longer based on what we do, but instead on Whose we are.

This doesn't mean we can't have ambitions, hopes, or goals in different areas of our lives; it simply means that we no longer need to be anxious or try to measure up. We are God's kids, and He will take care of us. We can rest.

One pastor has said, "We are sons and daughters of the King, so why do some of us live so underprivileged?" This doesn't mean that life should always be easy or that we will easily be successful or wealthy, but rather that we have the spiritual resources of heaven available to us to experience God's help, rest, and peace. We can go through our days with a hope and a joy that is unusual. When we spend our lives growing closer to the Lord, following His leading, and living for His glory, all of heaven is behind us.

We have the significance of a son or a daughter who is dearly loved.

Jesus, help me find comfort in the fact that I am a part of Your family, and I don't need to seek comfort anywhere else today.

—Matt Brown

COMPLETED

*Being confident of this, that he who began a
good work in you will carry it on to completion
until the day of Christ Jesus.*

—Philippians 1:6

God is leading the charge to finish His good work in our lives and to help us live out our faith. In fact, as Christians we don't work *for* victory, we work *from* victory.

The Gospel is not something you do; the Gospel is receiving something that's already been done for you. When Jesus gave His life on the cross for our sins, His final gasp was, "It is finished" (John 19:30). This means we no longer have to work for our salvation, or for God's approval. Rather, we live from God's approval. We are saved by God's grace alone, through faith alone, and true salvation always leads to God doing an amazing work inside of us. He carries the work "on to completion until the day of Christ Jesus" (Philippians 1:6).

D. L. Moody once had a man come up to him after a meeting who was distraught with how Moody was preaching the Gospel. "You don't tell people to do enough," the man said. Moody responded to the man, saying, "You have a two-letter religion, while I have a four-letter religion. Yours is 'You *do*.' Mine is 'Christ has already *done*.'"

Living out our faith from the finished work of Christ on the cross is freeing. We don't have to measure up, because He measured up for us. We live out our faith with copious amounts of joy and freedom because God has already finished the task.

Jesus, You are my victory. Help me to walk in it today, living from victory, even when I feel defeated.

—Matt Brown

EMPOWERED

*I also pray that you will understand the
incredible greatness of God's power for
us who believe him. This is the same mighty
power that raised Christ from the dead
and seated him in the place of honor at God's
right hand in the heavenly realms.*

—Ephesians 1:19–20 (NLT)

The apostle Paul wrote about God's "resurrection power" that is at work in us once we receive the Gospel. On a daily basis, God is working in us and giving us incredible power to help us follow Him. We may not always see it, and we may not always feel it, but it is there.

When we look back over our faith journey, we see more clearly how God has been working in us. But in the day to day, it can often feel as if we are not growing spiritually. Have you ever wondered how long you will struggle with the same sins or fears? Have you ever questioned why you can't seem to move past baby steps in your faith? Growth as a Christian is a common struggle for all of us because it often looks different than we expected or hoped.

When I was young, my family would go on an annual camping trip with extended family. It was always fun seeing our cousins. One year, I remember one of our cousins had changed drastically since we had been with him a year prior. He was taller and looked much older, and his voice had completely changed—it had gotten deeper. We were shocked at how much he had changed, but he and his family didn't understand our surprise. They had seen his change one day at a time. We were much more able to notice the changes because we hadn't been with him for a year. If you're discouraged by your growth, you may want to ask other believers in your life what they are seeing. Ask if people who have known you for a while see changes in you because of Christ.

This is how Christian growth happens. It is often years before we can truly say: "I may not be where I want to be, but thank God I am not where I used to be."

A friend once shared, "It is inconceivable to think that the same Spirit which raised Jesus from the dead would come into our lives and do nothing."

Even when we don't see it, even when we don't feel it, Christ is working in us to give us incredible power to follow Him.

Jesus, thank You so much for showing Your power in the midst of weakness on the cross, reminding me that You are strong in my weakness today.

—Matt Brown

ALIVE

He has delivered us from the domain of darkness and transferred us to the kingdom of his beloved Son, in whom we have redemption, the forgiveness of sins.

—Colossians 1:13–14 (ESV)

A few years ago, I was invited to visit an author's work in the Tenderloin district of San Francisco, where more than six thousand homeless inhabitants crowd a single city block.

It was awe-inspiring seeing their inner-city mission work, along with thousands of regular volunteers from local churches who intentionally love the broken, weary, strung-out people whom the world has given up on.

Through this mission, lives are being changed. Some of the people who were working with us on the streets had formerly lived on the streets themselves—strung out on drugs before Christ had changed everything for them through the Gospel.

My wife and I tagged on a few extra days to our trip to enjoy the sights and sounds of San Francisco. We enjoyed watching the iconic cable cars making their way up the winding hills and sipping flower tea at a nearby Chinatown restaurant. Several of the days, we made our way down to the Bay, where unbeknownst to us, America's Cup yacht races were taking place, along with an Olympic-sized footprint. There were lots of food stands, large screens, vendors, and activities taking place.

In one booth, I stopped to look at some nice brown leather shoes, and Michelle stopped at the booth next to it, and before I knew it, she was signing us up to enter a contest—for a free trip to Dubai from Emirates Airlines. We laughed at the idea but figured it was worth a shot.

Three months later we received an e-mail from a marketing company that looked like spam—it was claiming we had been selected for a free trip to Dubai. We slowly remembered we had signed up for the contest a few months earlier, and it took us a while to believe we had really won.

A month later, we made our way to Dubai and spent a few days in the fascinating, futuristic Middle

East city. Thanks to social media, we connected with a few Christian friends while we were there, including missionary acquaintances who pastor a church plant made up mostly of expats.

Several months after our visit, the missionary couple sent us a copy of the wife's new book. A few paragraphs she wrote forever changed my perspective about what the Gospel means:

> Being delivered from Satan, sin, and death is anything but average or boring. Having your sins forgiven and being redeemed and made alive is mind-boggling. The idea that anyone's testimony of blood-bought salvation could be uninteresting or unspectacular is a defamation of the work of Christ.
>
> Your testimony may have occurred in the most ordinary of circumstances, but behind the scenes a spiritual battle was taking place. The Holy Spirit of God peeled the scales from your spiritually blind eyes, awakened your soul to the bright light of the gospel in the face of Jesus Christ, and breathed life into your lifeless soul. God rescued you from the domain of darkness— however gilded or ordinary or innocent it seemed.

Then God transferred you into the kingdom of his beloved Son.

No testimony that involves the Son of God bearing your sins on the cross in order to bring you to God could ever be mundane or boring.[9]

Many Christians feel their testimony of coming to faith in Christ is boring. They have not done drugs or been an alcoholic or wasted away their lives in some terrible sin, so they don't feel they have an exciting faith story to share with others. But as she boldly wrote, the Bible begs to differ.

Paul said the same thing in Colossians 1:13–14: "He has delivered us from the domain of darkness and transferred us to the kingdom of his beloved Son, in whom we have redemption, the forgiveness of sins" (ESV).

Have you ever stopped to think about the epic that is the Gospel at work in your life? It rivals the best movies Hollywood can muster. In the Gospel, you haven't simply been made into a better person; you've been "delivered from the domain of darkness" (Colossians 1:13, ESV). We were "dead in [our] trespasses," and we've been "made alive together with him" (Colossians 2:13, ESV).

Use your gifts to help those in need, and keep your eyes open for all that God will teach you while you serve. Our story is no longer average or boring; it is spectacular because of what Jesus has done for us and in us. We were dead, and now we are alive.

Jesus, help me not only remember Your story of death and resurrection daily, but help me tell the story of how You have changed my life with boldness and compassion.

—Matt Brown

WEEK 4

THE GOSPEL
CHANGES OUR FUTURE

FAMILY

God decided in advance to adopt us into his own family by bringing us to himself through Jesus Christ. This is what he wanted to do, and it gave him great pleasure.

—Ephesians 1:5 (NLT)

In Christ, you have been adopted into a new family. The apostle Paul explained that Christians are people from diverse backgrounds who are now not only at peace with one another but have become blood-bought brothers and sisters. The Gospel brings people together like few things can. It causes people who would've never been in the same room together to love each other like family—because they are. Galatians 3:26 says, "For you are all children of God through faith in Christ Jesus" (NLT). The blood of Jesus that washes us is greater than our race, creed, nationality, ethnicity, or culture.

Love across social barriers brings glory to God because it is so rare outside the Church. Not every church in our country experiences the beauty of this kind of diversity, but our church near Minneapolis now has more than forty-seven nations of the world represented. God has done something unique in our community.

Our church was founded by my late grandfather-in-law. He emigrated from Canada in his twenties with his young wife. He left a good job at a bank for a financial position at a Bible college in Northern Missouri. He didn't find out until he arrived that the college was in financial ruins. He ended up becoming a traveling cookie salesman in the region. My grandmother-in-law says he was a great salesman, but I don't see how it could be hard to sell cookies. In addition to his full-time job, he pastored a small church that eventually had to close because people were leaving the small town. A church near Minneapolis was looking for their first pastor—it was just a group of families meeting in the basement of a home at the time. God clearly paved the way for him to lead the church. Four decades later, he retired at the church. The church had grown to thousands of weekend attendees and, under his leadership, had raised up countless young people into full-time ministry.

It wasn't until my grandfather-in-law was in his late seventies that one of his sons attempted to contact his father's birth family. My grandfather-in-law had been born out of wedlock, and his real parents had given him up for adoption. They had later married each other.

My wife and I went with other family members to meet his full sisters in Northern Canada—all of them in their late seventies. To our amazement, they not only looked like each other, they talked like each other and had similar mannerisms even though they hadn't met until their seventies! The same blood ran in their veins, and the same parents conceived them— they were family.

In Christ, even if our upbringings are completely opposite or we live worlds apart, you and I have been born into the same family through the Gospel of Jesus. If you've ever been on a mission trip or visited a church in another country (even another language), you feel this truth vividly—the same great sense of the presence of God, the same heart of worship, the same Bible preached and treasured in every faithful Christian church around the world.

So it doesn't matter what family you were born into— whether you are proud of your family or not; in Christ, we are all part of a beautiful, diverse family of God.

Jesus, Your resurrection invites me to live, talk, walk, and serve like You did; thank You for inviting me into Your family.

—Matt Brown

A NEW PEOPLE

Consequently, you are no longer foreigners and strangers, but fellow citizens with God's people and also members of his household, built on the foundation of the apostles and prophets, with Christ Jesus himself as the chief cornerstone.

—Ephesians 2:19–20

It was our second visit to the Holy Land. We had enjoyed a week of traveling all over the nation of Israel to the places where Jesus had walked and taught. Anyone who visits Israel cannot help but be amazed. There is so much history, so much of our collective faith packed into such a small part of the world. You could spend months there and still not see everything there is to see.

Near the end of our trip, we visited the port city of Joppa. This is the modern-day spot where at least two important stories in the Bible occurred. This is where

God spoke to Jonah, calling him to preach repentance to the people of Nineveh. You have to understand that the people of Nineveh in Jonah's day were the hated enemies of Israel. Jonah, in his own words, did not want them to repent. He did not want them to experience the compassionate mercy of God. He tried to run from the call of the Lord and was swallowed by a large fish. Eventually he was spit up onto the dry land of Nineveh, he preached repentance, and the city did repent—and God did relent.

Hundreds of years later, in this very same area, the apostle Peter was staying at the house of a friend. He went on the roof to pray, and God gave him a vision from heaven. He was told to eat unclean meats, but he refused. Like Jonah, he didn't want to do it. God used this vision to speak to him about the Gospel finally coming to the Gentiles. God was once again bringing His message of compassionate mercy to people outside the camp. He was telling the early church leaders that the Gospel was for *all* people, all over the world.

Paul told us in Ephesians 2 that when we receive the Gospel, no matter where we are from, we become a new people—citizens together of heaven. Not only do we become part of a new family, we become part of a new kingdom. In Christ, the lines that once divided us melt away as we are brought into one body under Him.

Jesus brings together people from every sphere of society as one new people to represent Him in the world.

Jesus, please lift my eyes to see I am not alone in celebrating Your love and victory on the cross. I'm kneeling shoulder to shoulder, together with millions upon millions all over the world.

—Matt Brown

VISION

For God, who said, "Let light shine out of
darkness," made his light shine in our hearts to
give us the light of the knowledge of God's glory
displayed in the face of Christ.

—2 Corinthians 4:6

Pastor Richard Wurmbrand told one of the most powerful stories I've ever heard. He led ministry to people
in persecuted nations around the world. Did you know
there are still people in dozens of nations around the
world today that don't have the freedom to worship
Christ like we do? If we listen to their stories, their faith
will inspire us and remind us to pray.

Wurmbrand once shared the Gospel with a Russian
captain. The man had never heard of Jesus before.

I read to him the Sermon on the Mount and the
parables of Jesus. After hearing them, he danced
around the room in rapturous joy, proclaiming,

"What a wonderful beauty! How could I live without knowing this Christ?" It was the first time that I saw someone jubilating in Christ.

Then I made a mistake. I read to him the passion and crucifixion of Christ, without having prepared him for this. He had not expected it. When he heard how Christ was beaten, how He was crucified, and that in the end He died, he fell in an armchair and began to weep bitterly. He had believed in a Savior and now his Savior was dead! . . .

Then I read to him the story of the resurrection. When he heard this wonderful news, that the Savior arose from the tomb, he slapped his knees, and shouted for joy: "He is alive! He is alive!" Again, he danced around the room, overwhelmed with happiness![10]

Maybe you didn't come to faith in Christ in this dramatic of a fashion, but the Bible tells us when we come to Christ, our spiritual eyes are suddenly opened, a veil is lifted, and the light of Christ shines on us.

This light is "the knowledge of God's glory . . . in the face of Christ" (2 Corinthians 4:6). When we receive the Gospel, we see everything differently. Our eyes are opened to see the glory of God, and seeing His glory changes everything in our lives. We see ourselves in proper perspective when our eyes are open to God's glory. And when we realize the glory of God, we are forever ruined for the things we lived for before. We can no longer direct our lives around ourselves; rather, we long to abandon everything to live for His kingdom purposes and glory.

Our spiritual vision is now clear. We were blind, but now we see.

Jesus, open the eyes of my heart to see Your eternal glory breaking out in the everyday moments of my life.

—Matt Brown

BRIGHT HOPE

The thief's purpose is to steal and kill and
destroy. My purpose is to give them
a rich and satisfying life.

—John 10:10 (NLT)

Adoniram Judson, the well-known missionary to India, once said, "The future is as bright as the promises of God." When we receive the Gospel, the future is always very bright, no matter what we face. I like to say it this way: *The future is as bright as the promises of God. And the promises in the Gospel are the brightest of all.* Our future is secure. In the words of evangelist Billy Graham, "I've read the last page of the Bible, and it's all going to turn out all right." Yes, and far more than all right!

Jesus said that He came to bring us into abundant life. What does that mean? There are lots of wrong ways to read that word *abundant.* We have to remember that Jesus's ultimate purpose on this earth was to die on the cross and then rise from the grave. Everyone who follows Him has been called both to carry our own cross and to one day be resurrected with Him forever.

Sometimes this life doesn't seem so bright, even as a Christian, but because of the Gospel, we always truly have a bright future.

I have a friend named Greg who has trained tens of thousands of young people around the country to share their hope in Jesus with others. He is like a walking Red Bull for God's glory. But he wasn't always so full of happiness, hope, and purpose. In fact, the trajectory of his life had been going in the opposite direction. But one day, God got ahold of his crazy Uncle Jack's life.

Uncle Jack was constantly in fights and in trouble with the police. He once even strangled two officers until they were unconscious while they tried to arrest him for assault. A suburban pastor sought him out and shared the Gospel with him. Uncle Jack came to Christ, and his faith led to much of the rest of Greg's troubled family coming to Christ as well. God transformed Greg's life as an eight-year-old and completely changed his future.

One day a youth worker told Greg that helping the poor is the point of the Gospel. Greg knew this wasn't fully true because he had lived in poverty and hopelessness as a child. He asked the youth worker, "Have you ever been poor?" The youth worker responded that he hadn't. Greg said, "Well, I grew up poor, and if you would've asked me as an eight-year-old whether I'd like all our bills paid or Jesus, I would've chosen Jesus every time." Countless poor Christians around the world would say the same thing.

This isn't to say we shouldn't help the poor—helping the poor is very close to God's heart, and it's an outworking of the Gospel in the heart of anyone who believes in Jesus—but it is not *the* Gospel. The Gospel is something far beyond how much or how little money we have or give on this earth. We have a bright future despite the circumstances we encounter, in the face of whatever pain and suffering we may have to endure, and no matter how much or how little financial resources we possess.

We have a bright future in Jesus. Because of the Gospel, the best is always yet to come.

Jesus, Your resurrection gives me hope that every dark thing will be swallowed up in life; help me hold fast to this hope today.

—Matt Brown

GAIN

But whatever were gains to me I now consider loss for the sake of Christ. What is more, I consider everything a loss because of the surpassing worth of knowing Christ Jesus my Lord, for whose sake I have lost all things. I consider them garbage, that I may gain Christ and be found in him, not having a righteousness of my own that comes from the law, but that which is through faith in Christ—the righteousness that comes from God on the basis of faith. I want to know Christ—yes, to know the power of his resurrection and participation in his sufferings, becoming like him in his death, and so, somehow, attaining to the resurrection from the dead.

—Philippians 3:7–11

I stood there face-to-face with a man who had given away many billions of his own hard-earned money to the kingdom of God. He started giving, and then giving some more, and slowly figured out a way to give away more than half of his income every year to get the Gospel to more people. He is one of the richest men in the world. He has encountered success that few people will ever know, yet he lives this quote by missionary C. T. Studd: "Only one life twill soon be past. Only what's done for Christ will last."

What could cause somebody to give away so much?

I read an article that said most people never feel rich enough. The vast majority of people feel like they need more money to be truly happy—whether they are small business owners, millionaires, or the super rich with tens or hundreds of millions of dollars in net worth. Everyone feels like they need just a little more, yet this billionaire dreams of giving more away. He has discovered something in the Gospel that we all need.

In the Gospel, we gain something so much greater than anything money can buy. Paul had experienced worldly success, intelligence, and notoriety in his community before finding Christ, yet he realized all his worldly gains were actually losses compared to the "surpassing greatness" of knowing Christ through the Gospel (Ephesians 1:19, NASB).

When you believe in Jesus, it is greater than your wildest dreams. Maybe you dream of being successful, famous, or wealthy. Maybe you dream of giving your life to serve the poor and making a real difference in this world. All your greatest dreams realized—selfish or altruistic—pale in comparison to what you already have in the Gospel once you have received Christ!

Your future in heaven, forever in God's presence, is secure. You can have incredible hope through any hardship or pain you face in this world. Paul wrote Ephesians *from prison*. Even though he was in chains and behind bars because of the Gospel, he wrote with great excitement about the very tangible joy, peace, and hope in the Gospel.

Whatever you hoped to gain before following Christ, now you gain God Himself. You now live your life near to God because of Christ. No gain could be greater. One pastor said, "The good news of the Gospel is that no matter your circumstances in this life, you get God."

Jesus told a story about the gain of the Gospel: "The kingdom of heaven is like treasure hidden in a field. When a man found it, he hid it again, and then in his joy went and sold all he had and bought that field" (Matthew 13:44).

The Gospel is worth everything we might pay to have it, and yet it comes to all of us free of charge. The Gospel is not simply a nice story—it is a treasure! It fills our hearts with so much joy that we will gladly lose everything to gain it.

And this is what Paul was trying to say in Philippians 3. His joy went far beyond the experience of earthly gain. And so Paul endured much pain and suffering and sacrifice to get the great hope of the Gospel to more people. He was more than happy to give of himself and endure hardship, suffering, threats, and loss because he had already gained so much in the Gospel.

In the same way, our joyful giving, our joyful sacrifice, and our joyful suffering show others the great gain of the Gospel.

Jesus, please help me remember You have already given me more than I could ever imagine.

—Matt Brown

28

VICTORIOUS

No, in all these things we are more than conquerors through him who loved us. For I am convinced that neither death nor life, neither angels nor demons, neither the present nor the future, nor any powers, neither height nor depth, nor anything else in all creation, will be able to separate us from the love of God that is in Christ Jesus.

—Romans 8:37–39

We often translate the Greek word *gospel* as "good news." It is a literal and helpful translation, but it is also woefully inadequate—far too pale to describe what God has done. When you think of "good news," you probably think of hearing that your favorite sports team won or a friend had a baby, or getting a good grade on an exam or a raise at work. Each of those is an example of good news, but the Gospel says something so much greater.

In the ancient world, tribes and people groups were often at war with neighboring tribes and people groups. When their army went out to war, the stakes could not be higher. If their army lost, it was not unusual for an enemy army to march into the city, force children into slavery, burn houses, rape women, and kill many of the elderly. The potential for absolute devastation loomed over every battle. The entire city would hold their breath, waiting for a herald to run from the battlefield with their fate.

If the army won, the runner would bring the precious message of victory, which was called "gospel." This is the word the Church uses to describe the death and resurrection of Jesus.

If, like those people groups, you spent weeks waiting—wondering whether you were going to be a slave, whether your children would be enslaved, whether your spouse would be abused or killed—your entire life would hinge on the report from the battlefield.

Likewise, the Gospel is way more than good news; it's a report of victory. The army of darkness has been defeated by Christ. Jesus won the battle that decides our eternity! We do not have to be slaves anymore. We don't have to work meaninglessly for the cruel masters of this world: performance, addiction, anxiety, bitterness, public approval, lust, pride, and money. We are free because we have won! This is much deeper and more powerful than our simple English understanding of "good news."

> *Jesus, thank You for winning the only battle that truly matters and bringing that victory to me. Help me to walk in that victory in every area of my daily life.*

> —Ryan Skoog

29

HEAVEN

But our citizenship is in heaven.
And we eagerly await a Savior from there,
the Lord Jesus Christ.

—Philippians 3:20

One of the greatest promises in the Gospel is that our eternal future in heaven is secure. This life is not the end. Jesus promises us that there is an eternal life beyond this short life. Because of our sin and shame, we deserved eternity in hell. The apostle Paul wrote, "Like the rest, we were by nature deserving of wrath. But because of his great love for us, God, who is rich in mercy, made us alive with Christ even when we were dead in transgressions—it is by grace you have been saved" (Ephesians 2:3–5).

God, in His great mercy, forgave us and redeemed us to Himself. He brought us into His own family. He gave us all these benefits in the Gospel, "in order that in the coming ages he might show the incomparable riches of his grace, expressed in his kindness to us in Christ Jesus" (Ephesians 2:7). We can never spend enough time studying this Gospel if God plans to spend all eternity showing us His goodness and His beauty!

I have a friend named Bruce who, during brain surgery, said he had a vision of heaven. He is a godly man, and a humble, faithful leader at his local church. He is soft-spoken, humble, faithful, and wise. I was astonished when he shared he had a vision of heaven and meeting Jesus during brain surgery. He said that there was no feeling on earth that could compare—he felt so much peace, love, and warmth.

He felt what it was like to be free from the weight of the sin of this world and said we don't recognize the weight of sin on earth because we are so used it. During his vision, Jesus came to him and said He still had things for him to do on earth and gave him three instructions: (1) Tell people I love them. (2) Show people I love them. (3) Teach people how to love again. Since Bruce reawakened after surgery, he has become a witnessing machine. He tells people about the love of Jesus wherever he goes on his routes doing dry cleaning. He has no fear and shares the Gospel with everyone he can.

Randy Alcorn wrote in his groundbreaking book on heaven,

Nothing is more often misdiagnosed than our homesickness for Heaven. We think that what we want is sex, drugs, alcohol, a new job, a raise, a doctorate, a spouse, a large-screen television, a new car, a cabin in the woods, a condo in Hawaii. What we really want is the person we were made for, Jesus, and the place we were made for, Heaven. Nothing less can satisfy us. . . .

For the Christian, death is not the end of adventure but a doorway from a world where dreams and adventures shrink, to a world where dreams and adventures forever expand.[11]

My friend Greg Laurie, a pastor and evangelist, said, "Take the most wonderful thing you have ever experienced in life, multiply it a million times, and you'll get a glimpse of what heaven's like."

Here on this earth, although the Gospel satisfies us like nothing else can, there will always be an ache within for the perfection of heaven. The Bible calls us "temporary residents and foreigners" on this earth (1 Peter 2:11, NLT). We were made for heaven, and we were made for God. So then, death is not the end. For the Christian, death is a graduation to something far, far better—all because of the Gospel.

Jesus, help me walk in all of the power of heaven today on this temporary earth. Help me practice resurrection. I can only imagine what it will be like in heaven one day with You.

—Matt Brown

NOW WHAT?

You are a letter from Christ . . . written not with ink but with the Spirit of the living God.

—2 Corinthians 3:3

The room held some of the world's greatest storytellers: internationally known viral filmmakers, award-winning photographers, best-selling authors, and other renowned artists. The topic of discussion was how to tell the Gospel in a way that would be fresh in our culture today.

Jesus wrote the most beautiful story of love and sacrifice. It's a timeless climax found in the very best of our literature—someone gives their life in love for someone else. From *Romeo and Juliet* to *Harry Potter* to *Star Wars*, the best stories end with the ultimate in personal sacrifice—the giving of one's own life for someone else.

Perhaps this resonates with so many, even those who do not believe in Christianity, because the Gospel was made to resonate deep in our hearts. This is the great metastory that makes sense of every other story. Jesus's story makes sense of each of our stories as well.

As the room of artists wrestled with the question, it became clear we don't need a new angle to the Gospel. The story still stands today on its own merits. Instead, we need to tell the million stories of how that old story intersects with individual lives—the story as it changes thieves into givers, the proud into servants, the hurt into healed, the selfish into sacrificers.

The poet Gerard Manley Hopkins wrote, "Christ plays in ten thousand places." Likewise, the Gospel story plays in *billions* of individual stories.

We defeat the darkness in today's world by telling how Christ plays out in our lives: "For the accuser of our brothers [Satan] has been thrown down . . . they have conquered him by the blood of the Lamb and by the word of their testimony" (Revelation 12:10–11, ESV).

"The blood of the Lamb" is the core of the Gospel. "The word of their testimony" is the stories of millions of lives changed by the Gospel.

Your story is powerful; it destroys darkness—not only in your life but in other people's lives. Whenever you share about your pain and healing, your testimony draws others with pain to the healing of the Gospel. Whenever you share about your brokenness and re-building, your testimony draws others with brokenness to the rebuilding aspects of the Gospel. Not everyone will believe your story, but they will believe that you believe it, and that is powerful—it can destroy what Satan is doing.

We have attempted to share the Gospel *and* share stories of the Gospel interacting with people's lives for this very reason.

Coca-Cola spends more than a billion dollars each year *not* to let you know Coca-Cola exists but to stay "top of mind" in your daily life. As you preach the Gospel to yourself daily, it wells up to "top of mind." It will naturally start spilling out into your daily interactions and conversations. Gratefulness, joy, peace, and Jesus will spill out of you.

Today, around 100,000 people will become Christians because the Gospel cannot be stopped or contained. Since that first Easter Sunday, the Gospel has been "bearing fruit and growing throughout the whole world" (Colossians 1:6). And as you see more of the beauty of the Gospel in your own life, it will become more beautiful to those around you. Someone around you might just be one of those 100,000 next week, next month, or next year.

Preaching the Gospel to your own soul every day might become the most important practice of your entire life.

Jesus, thank You for transforming the story of my life into an epic of grace. Help me boldly share what You have done in my life through my words, attitudes, and actions every day. Help me not let a day go by without sharing the Gospel with my own heart and with others.

—Ryan Skoog

ENDNOTES

1. Lee Strobel, *The Case for Christ* (Grand Rapids, MI: Zondervan, 1998).

2. Tolkien Gateway, "Eucatastrophe," http://tolkiengateway.net/wiki/Eucatastrophe, Letter 89.

3. Carsten Wrosch, Isabelle Bauer, Michael F. Scheier, "Regret and Quality of Life Across the Adult Life Span: The Influence of Disengagement and Available Future Goals," *Psychology and Aging* 20, no. 4 (2005): 657–670.

4. Wendell Berry, "Manifesto: The Mad Farmer Liberation Front" from *The Country of Marriage* (San Diego: Harcourt Brace Jovanovich, 1973).

5. James S. Bell Jr., ed., *The D. L. Moody Collection* (Chicago: Moody Bible Institute, 1997), 47–50.

6. Horatio G. Spafford, "It Is Well with My Soul," 1873.

7. Sigmund Freud, *Civilization and Its Discontents* (Austria: Internationaler Psychoanalytischer Verlag Wien, 1930).

8. Michael Card, *Matthew* (Downers Grove, IL: Inter-Varsity Press, 2013).

9. Gloria Furman, *Glimpses of Grace* (Wheaton, IL: Crossway, 2013), 65.

10. dc Talk and The Voice of the Martyrs, *Jesus Freaks: Martyrs* (Bloomington, MN: Bethany House Publishers, 1999), 202–203.

11. Randy Alcorn, *Heaven* (Carol Stream, IL: Tyndale, 2004), 160, 419.

ACKNOWLEDGMENTS

RYAN:

A guy named Bob Goff mistakenly took my aisle seat on an airplane. I didn't have the heart to tell him. On the plane ride he told me he was an author and I should write a book. So this book is largely a result of that flight. I never did tell Bob he accidentally took my seat. But he'll find out when he reads this.

I wake up most mornings and say, "Really?! I get to be with her?!"

Here are some people who have shaped these words—listed in very random order: Captain, Paul, Ma'am, Biff, Tom, Bishop Terry, Colones, Roger, Aaron, Syd the Kid, Linda, Princeton, Mark, Stephen, Brad, Raju, Colonel, Rosabell, Hannah, Matt, Alan, Brad, Rico, David, John, Bear, Anika, Madam Pres, Jerry, Brent, Micah, Tim, Willian, Fred, Kerry, Bill, Billy, U.S., Tommy, PD, Troy, Jesse, B&B, Skinner. I walk around in profound gratefulness to know you.

Jesus, I'm quite certain I could not have written about the Gospel without You. I wish I had a cymbal the size of a planet to crash in celebration of what You have done.

MATT:

I'm so glad I hadn't planned ahead and booked a car rental and hotel at a strategy meeting I was attending with Jamie Stahler. Because of that we became friends and spent hours enjoying conversation and talking life and ministry. And, of course, that led to this book together—seriously, such a privilege. Thank you for believing in this book from the beginning.

To the love of my life, Michelle, it's hard to believe it's possible to love you more than when we first got married thirteen years ago! You make my world go round. And to our boys, Caden and Jordan, who bring copious amounts of joy to our lives every day.

To Ryan Skoog, for your brilliant book idea that you shared with me, and for letting me be a part of it with you. This subject has been one of the primary passions of my life for years. I pray God uses this book to bless countless believers in the same way it has blessed us.

To Marshall Segal, for your incredible first edit of this book. We owe you more than we can say for your incredible skill and graciousness.

To Tia Smith, for your masterful editing work!

To Erica Chumbley, for your considerable work on this project. Thank you for guiding this to completion!

To Adam Weber, for your partnership on the curriculum side of this project. You are one of the most humble and gracious leaders I've ever met—so grateful for your friendship, brother!

ABOUT THE AUTHORS

RYAN SKOOG

Somehow, Ryan was able to marry Rachel, and they have two wild ginger-headed kids, Colin and Sydney.

Ryan lives at the intersection of entrepreneurship and missions. He has started several successful businesses, two of which—Fly for Good and Faith Ventures—help thousands of churches and ministries save on airfare and travel insurance for their mission trips.

He also started the nonprofit Venture.org with friends in college. Venture helps thousands of people around the world run, hike, bike, and swim to raise millions of dollars to help war refugees, trafficked children, and child soldiers in unreached areas of the world—serving 10,000 war refugee children and 682 girls rescued from trafficking every day. He has brought the Gospel to scores of countries from the shadows of Everest to the great rift valleys of Africa.

Ryan has an MBA in Entrepreneurship from Saint Thomas, serves on the Board of Brotherhood Mutual, and is an ordained minister with the Assemblies of God.

Ryan has also earned ninety-seven stitches from combining a deep love of adventure sports with a natural ability to be a klutz.

MATT BROWN

Matt (**@evangelistmatt**) is an evangelist, author, and founder of Think Eternity. He and his wife, Michelle, are impacting millions of people with the Gospel each year online and through live events. They also minister to more than two million followers on social media daily.

They have two sons, Caden and Jordan, and reside near the Twin Cities in Minnesota.